René Just Haüy

**An Essay on the Education of the Blind**

Dedicated to the King of France, Paris 1786

René Just Haüy

**An Essay on the Education of the Blind**
*Dedicated to the King of France, Paris 1786*

ISBN/EAN: 9783743407237

Manufactured in Europe, USA, Canada, Australia, Japa

Cover: Foto ©Thomas Meinert / pixelio.de

Manufactured and distributed by brebook publishing software
(www.brebook.com)

René Just Haüy

**An Essay on the Education of the Blind**

RE-PRINT, 1894

# A GUIDE

TO THE PROPER

## MANAGEMENT AND EDUCATION

OF

# BLIND CHILDREN

DURING THEIR EARLIER YEARS

(*Whether in their own family, in public schools, or under private teachers*)

### BY J. G. KNIE

Director of the School for the Blind at Breslau, Member of the Silesian Society for National
Improvement, and to whom was awarded the Medal of Merit, given by the Grand Duke
at Weimar

TRANSLATED BY

## THE REV. WILLIAM TAYLOR

S.C.L., F.R.S., F.R.A.S., M.R.I., Hon. Mem. R.S.S.A., Hon. Mem. R.S.S., Paris, &c.

*Who has added an Introduction and an Appendix*

### NEW EDITION

---

" Wie süss, wie schön ist es sie abzuwischen
Die Zähre, die des Dulder's Aug enstürzt "

KLEIN

---

LONDON : SIMPKIN, MARSHALL & CO
WORCESTER : DEIGHTON & SON, 53, HIGH STREET
PRINTERS AND PUBLISHERS
1861

LONDON
SAMPSON LOW, MARSTON & COMPANY
LIMITED
St. Dunstan's House
FETTER LANE, FLEET STREET, E.C.
1894

# NOTICE.

*As I have, for more than forty years, paid particular attention to the education and general treatment of the Blind, and, during that time visited many of the principal Blind Schools in Europe, I have had opportunity of examining their systems and management, and of ascertaining their practical results; and I am bound, in candour, to acknowledge that, in some respects, they are superior to most of the Institutions of a similar kind in England. On this subject many very valuable works have been published, both in French and German, but, I am sorry to say, that nothing of a* practical *nature has yet appeared in English (except a translation of Dr. Guillie's very useful book, "* ESSAI SUR L'INSTRUCTION DES AVEUGLES *"). This induced me to undertake the following Translation, which might have been more ably done by many others; but, as they have not done it, I thought it better to do it, even imperfectly, than that information so valuable and useful should not be made available in this country. The work is a little abridged, and some parts slightly altered to accord with our customs. And should this humble attempt to discharge a duty to the Blind (by publishing, in English,* KNIE's *useful little work) induce others, more qualified, to take up their cause, I shall feel that I have not laboured in vain; and I trust that the importance of the subject may, in some degree, atone for the imperfect manner in which it is now brought before the British public.*

W. T.

1861.

# TRANSLATOR'S INTRODUCTION.

The human race seems to have been subject to Blindness at all times and in all countries. The enthroned Monarch is no more exempt from it than the humblest of his subjects, for it spares neither age, sex, nor condition. To-day we gaze with delight upon the beauties of nature—to-morrow we may be deprived of that pleasure, and doomed to perpetual darkness,—even " amidst the blaze of noon."

What pen can describe the pang that rends a father's heart, when first he finds his child is blind ? Who can tell the feelings with which a tender mother presses to her heaving breast her sightless offspring ? She may weep o'er her babe, but her tears are not regarded—she may smile upon it, but her smile is not returned—her fond attempts to attract its notice fail ! 'Tis then the sting with greatest force is felt !

The Blind may be divided into two classes—those who were born blind, and those who have become blind after having seen. Very few are *born blind*, but numbers lose their sight in the early stages of their existence. Soon after birth infants are liable to inflammation of the eyes, and, formerly, many of those cases terminated in partial or total blindness, but, since the introduction of Vaccination and the improved mode of treatment, as well as to the increased facility with which the poorer classes can obtain Medical assistance, the cases of loss of sight have been greatly diminished. Still, in this country, upwards of 30,000 Blind persons were registered in the last Census ! Of this number no inconsiderable portion will, of course, be found amongst the wealthier classes ; but as they seldom move about, except in carriages, or under the guidance of friends, they are not so readily recognized as those who are led by a dog, or have to grope their way by help of a stick. This has given rise to the idea that very few blind are to be found among the rich. Doubtless the larger proportion occurs among the poor, as they are more exposed to accidents in factories, &c., and can less afford to seek the aid of the Oculist, than those in better circumstances.

When parents are unfortunate enough to have a blind child they seldom know what to do with it. The first impression is that it will never be able to do anything for itself, but will be a burden to them as long as it lives, and greatly mar their future happiness. When this case occurs to *poor* parents, who are, perhaps, engaged all day in the fields, or other employment from home, and cannot attend to their sightless offspring, it is often left, confined in a chair, throwing its legs and arms about, making grimaces, and acquiring habits which it will be difficult to eradicate, and which tend to give strangers an unfavourable opinion of its state of intellect. Whereas, if it were properly treated, and, when old enough, sent to any common school, it would improve in manner, and gather much information ; its mental faculties would have some chance of developing themselves, and it would be better prepared to receive further instruction. When the case happens to *rich* parents, *they*, likewise, are at a loss to know how to proceed with their little blind charge. The same dread of its being burthensome to them and a draw-back upon their happiness occurs to *them*, as it does to the poor ; and, indeed, with greater force ; since, for the *indigent* blind, there are many schools, where they may be taught to earn much, if not the whole, of their own livelihood ; whilst for those in the *wealthier* classes, there is, in this country, unfortunately, no place where they can receive an education, suitable to their station in life, and experienced Tutors of the Blind are seldom to be procured. No wonder, then, that parents—whether rich or poor—who have blind children, should, at first, be a little cast down at the prospect before them. But it is the object of the following pages to enliven those prospects, and to console and cheer such parents, by furnishing them with a few plain instructions to guide them in the treatment of their blind children, at least during the first years of their life. It would be well for those parents to visit Schools for the Blind, and see what is there done by the pupils. And if they would read the accounts of some of the numerous blind persons who have arrived at the highest eminence in science and literature, and have been not only a credit to themselves, but a comfort to their friends, and valuable members of society (see Appendix), it would afford them great consolation, and encourage them to regard, with resignation and composure, their little blind charge, and to watch, with affectionate interest, the development of its mental and bodily powers. And should it, hereafter, eminently distinguish itself, as so many have done, how sweet would, then, be the reward for all their parental care and anxiety ! This little work is not merely a statement of theoretical speculations, but the result of long experience and close observation. KNIE (the Author), who is himself blind, is highly educated, and has been Director of the Institution for the Blind, at Breslau, since the year 1821. His School is so admirably and advantageously conducted, that it is looked upon as a *model* School for the country round it, even to the distance of many leagues, and is greatly patronized by the neighbouring Powers.

Till within about seventy or eighty years, the blind were thought to be incapable of acquiring any great degree of useful knowledge ; now, however, experience has shewn that there is scarcely any branch of education beyond their reach. All Blind persons—except idiots—may be taught enough to lessen their affliction, if not to make them useful and happy. And by help of embossed printing, and the many ingenious contrivances used in teaching the Blind, the difference, between them and their seeing brethren, is now reduced almost to a minimum.

The Blind, as well as others, have an undoubted claim to be educated, but the amount of their education must depend upon many things. Formerly it was thought they could be taught only in schools for the blind, where proper tools and teachers are provided for them, but, now the subject is better understood, they may be partially, if not entirely, educated in their own family circle.

Many people, when they are in company where there is a Blind person, often keep aloof from him, not from any want of kindiy feeling, but merely from not knowing how to address him. They would do well to talk to him, just as if he had his sight,—not ask him if he has *heard* such and such a book read, &c., as that would remind him of his misfortune, and give him pain ; but say, " Have you *read* such and such a book ? Have you *seen* Mr. B— to-day ? " and such like. This mode of addressing him gives him the comfortable feeling that there is nothing, so very peculiar, about him as to remind them that he is blind. In short, "Treat him, as far as possible, in the same manner as you would those possessing sight." Zöllner says (" *Unterhaltung ueber die Erde,*" &c., Band v., S. 576), " I have never yet known a Blind person who had been respectably brought up, and tolerably educated, whose character was not amiable, and in whose society I did not feel pleasure."—Knie is a good classical scholar and tolerable mathematician, and has translated into his own language (German) several works from the Latin, French, Italian, &c. A young man in London (Fred. Clark) has, with his own hand, and his own press, printed, in relief and in the common Roman letter, a Latin Dictionary, for the use of the Blind ; but, unfortunately, only seven copies were struck off, so that the work must be very scarce, and may be looked upon as a literary curiosity. He has since gone to America, where he hopes to obtain employment in giving lessons in Mathematics, even up to the Differential Calculus ! Such a case has not occurred, in this country, since the time of Saunderson, who, though Blind, was Professor of Mathematics in the University of Cambridge, and recommended to that office by Sir I. Newton.

It is to be regretted that there is, in the English language, no *practical* treatise on the education and general management of the Blind, except a translation of Dr. Guillie's admirable work, " *Essai sur l'Instruction des Aveugles.*" This circumstance will contribute much towards rendering KNIE'S book acceptable, as containing, in a small space, much valuable information, which cannot fail to be highly useful to those who have the care of Blind children, and who may never have seen *how* or *what* they are taught, in the various schools for the Blind, or what they are capable of learning. Tracts, containing information of this kind, are distributed, gratis, in Prussia, Austria, &c., and greatly tend to rescue many a sightless sufferer from a life of indolence and misery, and to relieve the parents from the painful feeling that their Blind child must be a burden to them through life.

Jäger says (" *Ueber die Behandlung, welche blinden und taubstummen Kindern, hauptsaechlich bis zu ihrem achten Lebensjahre, in Kreise ihrer Familien an ihren Wohnorten ueberhaupt zu theile werden sollte* "), " No greater benefit can be done to a Blind child than to accustom him, as soon as possible, to do everything he can for himself ; and first of all to move alone, from one place to another."

Much has been said about the loss of one sense being compensated for by the improvement of the remaining ones. No doubt, where *four* senses have to do the duty of *five*, they must be more frequently called into action, and thus improved, or rendered more acute, by practice. A Blind man (Jacob Birrer) was asked if he thought, when one sense was lost, that the others were proportionately strengthened ? To which he answered, " If there are five pipes conveying water from a fountain, and you stop one of them, will the water flow any more readily through the other four ? "

There is a very common notion that the Blind can " *feel* colours." No doubt they can tell the difference between a basket twig that is not coloured and one that is, where the colouring matter has caused the surface to feel more or less rough. Also, some colours render cloth more harsh to the touch than others, and sometimes have a peculiar smell, and the Blind make great use of their olfactories in distinguishing one thing from another. But if you give them glass, feathers, petals of flowers, &c., they can tell nothing about the colour of them. Spread a silk handkerchief upon the table, and let them put their hands upon it, and ask them if it is of *one* colour or of *many ?* If they say " many," ask what they are, and request them to trace, with the finger, the boundary of each (which they can easily do, *if they can distinguish one colour from another, by the touch*), and you will soon discover that " feeling colours " is altogether a fallacy. Their hands have been placed in coloured water, but in no case did they tell what the colour was. Care must be taken, in these experiments, to bandage well their eyes, for, if they have the least glimmer of sight, they can distinguish *colours*, though not *forms*. They will sometimes undertake to tell colours by the touch, even in a dark room, where there can be no colour. I mention this because there are disreputable Blind persons who, for the sake of obtaining money, endeavour to impose upon the unsuspecting by pretending to distinguish colours by the touch. Some years ago, a girl undertook to tell the colour of bits of silk, cloth, &c., when put into a bottle, she only feeling the outside of it. And, strange to say, there were persons who paid their own power of investigation so ill a compliment as to believe it!! A clever Blind young man, at Zurich, when asked if he could feel colours, answered, "No!— it is impossible for a Blind person to *feel colours*. The colouring matter sometimes makes the surface of the thing coloured more or less rough, and *that* we can feel, but more than one colour may produce the same degree of roughness."

Those who are interested in the treatment and education of the Blind will do well to consult the various works mentioned in the Appendix, as they afford every information relating to this subject, especially the "*Lehrbuch zum Unterrichte der Blinden*," by Klein, of Vienna, whose penetration, sound judgment, and fifty years' experience must give great weight to his opinion.

In pursuing this subject, I now come to a case which cannot fail to touch every feeling heart, and excite the compassion of every humane mind—I mean the case, which not unfrequently occurs, of a child being born, or becoming, not only *Blind*, but also *Deaf*, and, consequently, *Dumb*—there being no case recorded (as far as I know) of congenital deafness being unaccompanied by the consequent want of speech.—Reader, I ask you to pause and contemplate so lamentable a case. A human being doomed to drag out his existence in perpetual darkness and perpetual silence, never to see an approving smile—never to hear a consoling word! But, even in this extreme case, there is a ray of comfort for the afflicted parents. For by the embossed printing, the various and ingenious contrivances for facilitating the education of the Blind, and the improved methods of instruction, even these unfortunates are often taught to read, write, to do work of various kinds, and, apparently, to feel comfortable, if not happy! Let those who have children, blessed with all their senses, consider this, and be thankful.

It is much more difficult, in these cases, for parents to know what to do, or how to ascertain the best mode of treating such helpless objects. Many persons are acquainted with the case of Laura Bridgeman, Deaf and Dumb, and Blind, who has long been under the care of that talented and excellent friend to the sightless, Dr. Howe, at Boston, U.S. She has, through his skilful management and judicious instruction, acquired so much information, on various subjects, as to astonish all who have seen her. Other cases of this kind occur at Philadelphia, Bruges, Lausanne, Stuttgart, &c., and also in Great Britain. The one at Bruges is a female, in the Institution which the judicious and indefatigable Abbé Carton directs, with so much credit to himself and benefit to the pupils. In a very few months she learned to knit, even fancy knitting, and was able to distinguish the letters of the alphabet embossed on paper or card. When I saw her she appeared very happy, and always seemed pleased when the Abbé took hold of her hand. The sense of *touch* may be said to be the only inlet through which information or instruction can be conveyed to beings so unfortunately circumstanced. How desirable, then, is it so to cultivate that sense, as to make it a means of communicating such information to these afflicted objects, as may, in some degree at least, associate them with their seeing brethren!

Much has been said and done (in this country chiefly, for it is very little patronized on the Continent or in America) respecting *Arbitrary* Alphabets in embossing books for the use of the Blind. Unfortunately we have, in Great Britain, several such alphabets in use in different Institutions, and the advocates of one system oppose those of others, with a hostility which is neither complimentary to their judgment nor to their benevolence. For whatever tends (as all arbitrary alphabets do when used as a means of education) to separate the Blind from the seeing, in their social intercourse with them, must, of necessity, be hostile to their best interests, because it lessens their opportunities of obtaining assistance from others. Fancy a fellow creature enshrouded in perpetual darkness, deaf to every sound, and unable to give utterance either to his feelings or his wants, and then say whether he should be taught the common alphabet, known to all, or an arbitrary character, known only to a very few? This point I may safely leave to any unprejudiced person. The Blind should be EDUCATED *by means of the alphabet in common use with those who see,* and afterwards they may, for amusement or information, learn any alphabet invented for them. As opinion should always give way to fact, take the case of one blind and deaf and dumb. How can information be conveyed to him except through the sense of touch? If he has been taught the common alphabet, any one, by writing with the finger upon his hand or back, may communicate some cheerful sentence to relieve the monotony of his gloomy existence, but, if he has been taught only an *arbitrary* character, no one, who has not learnt it, can communicate with him ; and as he may probably, after leaving the school, never meet with any one who understands his system, he is, therefore, deprived of that advantage which a knowledge of the common alphabet would afford him. This is a cruelty we have no moral right to inflict.

In the report of the Jurors at the Great Exhibition, vol. ii., page 918, is the following :—" *Mr. Friedlander repeats the* UNANSWERABLE *arguments against the adoption of arbitrary characters and stenographic or phonetic systems, and strongly recommends the use of our own alphabet.*"

# PREFATORY REMARKS,

## BY THE AUTHOR.

*As I have written no particular Preface, I feel it necessary here to remark that the following (fourth) edition of this work (as well as the first and second) is printed at the cost of the Prussian Authorities, and that is the reason why it has not appeared in the shops of the booksellers.*

*In drawing up several of the sections of this fourth edition, especially that relating to music, I have thankfully availed myself of the very valuable remarks of my friends, Ernest Koblitz and Albert Kienel.*

J. K.

---

*Note—the words between [ ] and the foot-notes are by the Translator.*

*Some passages, on account of their importance, occur twice, such as the articles mentioned in page 28, which are nearly repeated in page 40; but the one is in Knie's work and the other in the Appendix.*

# A GUIDE

## MANAGEMENT AND INSTRUCTION

OF

# BLIND CHILDREN.

---

*Section I.*

THE erroneous idea which many, who have their sight, entertain, that children who are born blind, or who have lost their sight at a very early age, are incapable of receiving instruction, has frequently occasioned either the most culpable neglect or the most absurd treatment of such unfortunate children, and when they are afterwards received into Schools for the Blind, sometimes presents, to the teachers, greater difficulties than even the blindness itself, and not unfrequently prevents the accomplishment of the object in view, or, at least, renders it painfully tedious. Hence, about the year 1830, the Silesian Association for Instructing the Blind, felt it their duty, to the parents and teachers of blind children, to print and distribute, gratis, throughout Silesia, a short Guide, or instructions, for the use of such as might have the management or education of those sightless unfortunates. The happy results of this step have clearly shown themselves in the progress made in learning, by such pupils, when afterwards received into our Institutions for the Blind ; whereas, on the other hand, many Blind children, whose parents had no knowledge of these Instructions, were found in the most deplorable state of ignorance when brought to the schools, even at seventeen or eighteen years of age. In 1837 a member of the Prussian Government caused, at his own cost, a new and enlarged edition to be distributed, gratis, through the Prussian provinces. In 1839 a third edition was published and distributed, at the cost of the State. But, as the parents and relations of Blind children, for whose benefit they are intended, belong, for the most part, to the humbler classes, and therefore seldom read such things, it is particularly requested that all who have it in their power—especially the clergy—in places where there are Blind children, will not only call the attention of those who have the care of them to these instructions, but also endeavour to explain and enforce them in such manner as to render them as serviceable as possible in promoting the welfare of a class of our fellow creatures who have so large a claim upon the sympathy and assistance of their more fortunate brethren.

## Section II.—*The Treatment of Infants.*

THE mind of a child is capable, at a very early period of its life, of receiving impressions and forming ideas of external objects through the sense of vision. Even in the mother's arms it soon distinguishes her smile, and gives expressions of joy or dislike at the things it *sees*. But very few of these operations of the mind evince themselves in a blind child, the parents of which look in vain for it to smile upon them, or shew any desire to take hold of things presented to it. [Oh ! who can tell the pang which rends the father's heart on discovering that his child is blind ? Who can describe the feelings with which the fond mother presses to her heaving bosom her sightless offspring ? or who can conceive a yearning parent's anxieties for its future welfare ?] In bringing up blind children the remaining senses should be most carefully cultivated, in order to compensate, as far as possible, for the one which they have not ; and this can now, through the help of the many ingenious contrivances for facilitating the education of the Blind, be done to a great extent by the sense of touch, which, in things that can be handled, will go far to supply the loss of sight. The Blind must *handle* objects, in order to acquire a knowledge of their form, &c., and for this purpose the *ends* of the fingers serve best. The *colours* of various substances can be known by the *sight alone*. Therefore the parents of blind children, in order to prevent their faculties or mind remaining inactive, should especially attend to the senses of *touch* and *hearing*, and put into the hands of their children all such things as they may handle and examine without danger. Things differing in form and quality should be constantly given and exchanged, one for the other, and the characteristic differences pointed out. At one time give them *rough* things, at another *smooth*, *angled*, *round*, *hard*, *soft*, *&c.* For example, wood, fruit, cloth, money, children's playthings, especially bells, rattles, drums, trumpets, &c., afterwards models of animals, machines and such like. At the same time they should be conversed with and instructed in a mild and kind manner. Children who have their sight perceive the love of their parents in their looks and gestures—the Blind become sensible of it from the tone of the voice, but not in lamentation over their misfortune. It is a cruel sympathy for the Blind, who do not know the extent of their deprivation, to be constantly reminding them of it by useless expressions of pity and compassion. Furthermore, it is advisable to sing to them, and when an instrument can be had, to play to them some simple, soft, and pleasing melody ; for thereby the *ear* is formed and a taste for music awakened in the child before it can utter a note or musical sound. In this manner the organs of speech and the power of thinking will be as readily developed in a blind child as in one who can see.

*Section III.—Treatment after the first Year or two.*

Now comes the rule to be observed, THAT BLIND CHILDREN SHOULD BE TREATED, AS FAR AS POSSIBLE, IN THE SAME WAY AS THOSE WHO HAVE THEIR SIGHT,—except in some few particulars peculiar to their situation.

They should be taught to understand and name the different parts of the body and limbs, and the uses of them. To this knowledge of themselves should be added that of the furniture in the room, &c. They must not be allowed to pass their time in sitting still or being idle, for thereby they lose the opportunity of acquiring any knowledge of the objects around them, or of learning to move cleverly and cautiously from place to place. It is a mistaken kindness to carry blind children about, more than those who have their sight, or to guide them farther or beyond what is necessary ; for when they come to walk or play, and expect direction or assistance from others (no one, perhaps, being present), they may injure themselves or the things around them. To be constantly inactive is injurious both to their mind and body.

*Section IV.—Learning to walk, &c.*

BLIND children learn to walk as soon as those who see, but it is necessary, at first, to guide them a little more, and shew them how high to lift their feet, &c., for they often get a habit either of lifting them very high or scarcely lifting them at all. Attention should also be paid to their turning out their toes properly, for which purpose it will be well, every day, to make them stand awhile in the proper position, as soldiers do at drill. Furthermore, it is necessary to accustom them, in going about, to hold one hand (the left generally) across before their breast, in order to guard them against danger from open doors, &c., the other feeling below for such things as tables, chairs, &c. The body should be erect and the head well up, in no wise to lean forward, as is often the case with the *neglected* Blind, who, at first, from timidity, frequently confine their movements to turning round in nearly the same spot. They should, therefore, be taught to go about the room and examine such of the furniture, &c., as may be in it, and left *as much as possible to shift for themselves.* Place them in one part of the room and direct them to make their way to some other, endeavouring to guard *themselves* against injury from such things as may arrest their progress. This will teach them caution. When the child has become acquainted with the room he generally inhabits, take him, by degrees, to other parts of the house, and even to the garden or neighbouring places, and let him endeavour to find his way back to the place he had left, and with as little assistance as possible. With very young children it is best, in teaching them to go about, first to lead them by the hand ; afterwards, let them take hold of one end of a *stick*, the teacher holding the other—this tends to increase their confidence. Then do the same by a *string*, which, from its flexibility, is not so good a guide as the stick, and consequently teaches them to depend more upon themselves. Next let them try to follow the teacher about by listening to the sound of his feet, and then they will soon be able to move carefully without any assistance. Going up and down stairs requires particular attention. He should be directed not to change his feet upon the same step, but to place the moving foot upon the next step, and to hold fast by the rail or banister. It is not good—except for very young children—to give signals to guide them, because they would feel the want of them when they went to strange places, where none would be given. By moving about *slowly* at first they acquire confidence, and thereby the sooner become able to go more quickly, according to the old proverb, " Eile mit weile,"—" Hasten slowly."—If in difficulty or doubt, when they are walking, the safest way is to set the toe down first, and then the heel, making good each step before taking another. In the same cautious manner he should be taught, as he gets older, to find his way to the house of some neighbour, to some field, &c., and then it will be well for him to carry in his hand a light switch or walking stick, with which to feel his way and prevent his falling into a pit or ditch ; or going against anything that may hurt him, or over which he might stumble. When a blind person is taken to places or roads, with which he is *not well* acquainted, let him take hold of the guide's arm,—not the guide his—keeping a quarter of a step, as it were, behind him. He will thus feel the motion of his leader, and should be taught to "keep step with him." In crossing water by narrow bridges or planks, the guide should go first, holding him by one hand, directing him to examine, with his stick, the breadth of the bridge as he proceeds, always keeping his stick touching one side, and he will thus pass over safely. (This and the following rules apply also to those who have become blind in later life, who, through timidity, are often more helpless than those who were born blind.)

When a blind person attempts to sit down, he should first feel the seat with his hand, not only to ascertain its true position, but, also, to discover if anything be upon it, which he should carefully remove, and then sit slowly down. When he bows or stoops down, it is best first to draw back one foot a little, in order to stand firm, and then place one hand before his chin to prevent his coming in contact with a table, the back of a chair, &c., which he may not be aware of. By practice and observation a blind person will be able, by the impulse of the air upon his face, &c., or by the difference in the sound of his feet, to ascertain when he approaches any person, or thing as large as, or larger than himself, and even to form some idea of its size.

---

*Section V.—The Use of the Hands and Sense of Touch.*

THE *hands* of a blind person must, in numerous cases, serve him for *eyes*, therefore a *skilful use of them* is of the greatest importance. Should this be neglected in early years it is often impossible to *acquire* it afterwards. The hands which have long been unaccustomed to do anything become weak and soft, the bones thin, and the fingers so loose, as it were, that they might in some cases be turned back to touch the wrist, because the flexor muscles have never been called into strong action. Such neglected children are not only unfit for *hand work*, or mechanical operations, but also, from not being accustomed to make any good use of the sense of touch, are scarcely capable of applying it to feeling embossed maps, to reading from raised letters, &c., without very great labour and patience on the part of the teacher. And this difficulty is often increased by the neglected state of the *mind*, which is, generally, in such children, equal to that of the *body*, although they may possess first-rate abilities, which, for want of development, lie useless. It is, therefore, highly necessary that blind children should, from their earliest years, be well accustomed to the use of their hands and of their powers of observation. For this purpose let them have all sorts of toys, &c., and think not that the Blind have no pleasure in such things, because they do not *see* them. In this way they first learn the use of their hands, and by dressing and undressing dolls, girls learn to dress and undress themselves, and to understand the different parts of their dress. Let them have an opportunity of feeling different sorts of fruits, vegetables, &c., and as they are changed, one for another, the difference pointed out, such as their shape, hardness or softness, weight, roughness, or smoothness, taste, smell, &c. Such things, in a dry state, should be kept in little boxes, where they can often be referred to. Amongst these should be several things of the same *form* but differing in *material*, others of the same *material* but differing in *form*. Such a collection should contain something of all sorts—balls and dice, of glass, ivory, wood, metal, &c.—wire of various kinds and sizes ; things made of horn, leather, pasteboard, &c.—seeds of plants, flowers (such as will dry), pieces of wood of different kinds. Cloth of silk, linen, cotton, woollen, &c. Feathers, hair, fur, bristles, scales of fishes, when not too small ; cord, buttons, hooks, bits of iron, brass, lead, tin, copper, zinc, &c., rough and polished ; also coins of various kinds. The child should be taught to select some of these according to their *form*, others according to their *material*, and that may be done by way of amusement. Something relating to their use, substance, construction, &c., should, at the same time, be stated by the teacher, and afterwards required of the pupil.

When children show an enquiring mind, they should in no way be checked, but, on the contrary, encouraged by the teacher to ask numerous questions, although he may sometimes be under the necessity of giving for answer, " I, myself, do not exactly know." Should he be detected in pretending to know things, which he really does not, or in giving evasive answers to conceal his ignorance, he will lose the confidence of his blind pupil. The child must be well practised in counting from 1 to 100, forwards and backwards (let not this latter be neglected), and in the multiplication table ; also in mental arithmetic, which is a most valuable exercise for the mind. He should be taught to measure the length, breadth, and depth of various things ; and till he can use a rule with notches or pins to mark the divisions, a string with knots of different sizes, half-an-inch or an inch apart, may be employed. Also he should be taught the weight of things, and the use of scales, steelyards, &c. He would learn that things of the same weight and form might differ in size, on account of the nature of the substance of which they are made, &c. As scales and weights can be found in almost every house, it will not be necessary to shew how they may be explained (when not at hand) by a stick, balanced in the middle, between the thumb and finger, &c. The thickness and strength of string, thread, &c., should not be omitted. Models, of houses, churches, mills, carriages, ships, &c., and of other things too large to be examined by the hand ; also of ferocious animals, venomous reptiles, &c., should be plentifully supplied. By frequent and close examination of these things, his touch will become more certain in its indications, and his fingers acquire that strength and activity, which to him are indispensable. It is desirable to preserve the ends of the fingers as much as possible from injury, as they are to supply, as far as may be, the place of eyes. That the Blind can distinguish colours by the touch is altogether an erroneous idea. Colour is the effect of the rays of light, and therefore not perceivable by the touch. In the dark there is no colour. Certain things may be distinguished by the Blind, according to the colour, when the colouring matter has altered the nature of the surface or texture of the thing coloured ; but for this distinction they are indebted to the roughness, smoothness, harshness, &c., caused by the pigment, and not to the reflected rays of light. Thus the Blind easily deceive themselves by taking that for colour which is really not so.

### Section VI.—*Use of the Taste and Smell.*

Not only the sense of touch, or feeling by the finger end, is to be practised by the Blind, but also the senses of Taste and Smell, so that they may be able, not merely to say this or that thing tastes sweet or sour, salt or bitter ; and that others smell agreeably or unpleasantly, are fragrant or pungent ; but should be able so far to distinguish things, as to say, at once, this is sugar, vinegar, lemon, wine, beer, honey, sulphur, tobacco, snuff, soap, wax, tallow, cheese, &c. Further, their attention should be directed to the *taste* of different metals, such as gold, silver, copper, tin, &c., and to such things as clay, which, when unburnt, will adhere to the tongue, and when breathed upon, emit a faint odour, &c.

### Section VII.—*The use of the Sense of Hearing.*

The sense of Hearing, in the Blind, must be *particularly* cultivated. Not every blind child has so much discernment as, of itself, to distinguish the sounds of different things, such as that of a knife, money, wood, stone, &c., when it falls to the ground, but he will soon learn to distinguish the value of different pieces of money by the sound. The sound of things sliding upon, or rubbing against others, also the buzzing of various insects, the noises of domestic and other animals, birds, etc., should be noticed. The possession of a singing bird is generally interesting and amusing to the Blind, and not altogether useless. There is a sprightliness in the singing of a bird which cheers them. Attention should be directed to the noise made by the *movement* of animals, persons, &c., and that it is different in small and large rooms. The size of any room may be well judged of, by speaking in it, also its height, length, and breadth, and whether furnished or not. Also the distance of a speaker, by the sound of the voice.—This can be practised by removing to different distances from the speaker, &c. A well-educated ear will enable the Blind, not only to guess the height of a person who speaks to him, but to form some--not unfrequently, correct—idea of his character. As the *countenance* is the "mirror of the mind," to those who see, so is the *voice* to the Blind. But far different from the cultivation of the ear, for general purposes, is that training of it for *music*, since the talent or taste for that art is not possessed in the same degree by all. Playing or singing to Blind children simple airs, as was before stated, will best suit for the beginning, but for the further development of that talent, methodical and regular musical instruction will be necessary.

### Section VIII.—*On Dressing and Undressing, Feeding themselves, &c.*

The blind child should be taught, as soon as possible, to dress and undress himself, to button, tie knots of various kinds, both fast

C

and slip, or loop knots, and if this be well practised daily, for about a quarter of an hour or so, it will soon prove to be no waste of time, as some unthinking parents suppose, who for years together, through mistaken kindness, dress and undress their blind children, instead of teaching them to do it for themselves, and then complain that God has laid upon them so heavy an affliction, while the fault, in *this particular*, at least, is their own, and the remedy within their power. The clothing, especially of the girls, should be made in the plainest and simplest manner, so that nothing should be tied or fastened on the *back*, as that greatly increases the difficulty of putting them on and off without assistance, and hooks or buttons should be used rather than pins. The folding of neckcloths, pocket-handkerchiefs, aprons, and other linen may be first taught by practising upon paper. The clothes, when taken off, should always be carefully laid one upon another, so that they may be readily found when they are again to be put on. *In these and all other operations, the greatest order should be strongly inculcated*, for that which is desirable in all, is doubly necessary and beneficial for the Blind. Even so should the child be taught to feed himself with a spoon, then with a fork, and, lastly, with a knife, in addition ; and to observe the greatest cleanliness possible. First a deep plate or dish should be used, which must be held by the edge in the left hand, or rather the hand laid upon the flat edge, to prevent the contents being pushed off it by the spoon, fork, or knife, which he must hold in the right hand. And when the plate is nearly empty, it must, by the left hand, be raised a little on one side, and the fragments gathered together with the spoon or fork in the right, so as to be more easily found and taken up. Clever children can easily be taught to use dexterously the spoon, fork, and knife. It is much to be recommended that a small plate or saucer be placed near, on which bones, stones of fruit, &c., may be put, as it is not easy for the Blind to avoid taking them up a second time, when left upon the same plate ; nor can they easily, as the seeing do, place them round the edge of their plate. The Blind may be readily taught to help themselves to such drinkables as are *cold*, for as they pour them into a glass, they will feel the cold increase upwards as the glass fills : moreover, the weight and sound of the liquor, as it gets nearer to the top, will assist much, if attended to. The Blind should be taught to serve themselves, as much as possible, *in everything*. In many of these necessary manipulations they will often receive assistance from those around them, and when any one, who has his sight, is about to teach the Blind, he would often derive considerable advantage by first trying the experiment with his own eyes shut.

## Section IX.—*The use of the Memory and of the Intellect.*

THE exercise of the memory should be neglected in no child, but especially in the *Blind*, for *they* cannot, like those who see, have recourse to books, or written memorandums to assist them. Also, a naturally weak memory can, by practice, become tolerably strong, retentive and exact. In order to accomplish this end in the Blind, the memory must be gradually and accurately led on, from things well known, to things unknown, else that evil—a dislike to learning—will arise, especially in the young. It is also necessary that they be taught the right use and meaning of words ; for, if children acquire a bad pronunciation, or wrong meaning of a word, it will not easily be corrected. Interesting anecdotes, and well-selected poetry, may be constantly read or related to them, with great advantage, but what is called " nonsense " should be avoided. Something new should be taught every day, and some of the former day's lessons repeated. More extended repetitions should be made weekly, and, perhaps, monthly. The proverb that " Repetition is the mother of knowledge," used to be considered a golden rule ; and a *quick* memory can become a *retentive* and *true* one, only by repetition.

In beginning to exercise the memory, the teacher should choose short and easily understood sentences, which may be made to operate beneficially upon the heart and mind, and may be illustrated by fit examples and simple narratives. Verses or sentences out of the Bible, or Prayer Book, may be selected ; also fables, parables, histories, &c., especially such as are in rhyme, as they are more easily fixed in the memory. Preference should be given to such passages as inculcate trust in the providence of God, contentment under His dispensations, the advantages of virtuous conduct, and a stedfast hope in a better life after this. These should be impressed upon the memory by frequent repetition. It is doubly important that the Blind should have their minds well stored with religious maxims and subjects, as they have not the same advantage of referring to books as they have who see, and therefore need it the more. Ballads and epic poems are generally interesting and instructive. For the understanding of more refined language, the best plan is to read to the pupils short narratives and descriptions, only from point to point, they repeating each portion read, till the whole shall have been gone through, then read the whole again, without interruption. Avoid setting before the Blind things which, on account of their age, or state, would be beyond their comprehension, and let all explanations be clear and understood, lest a wrong impression be formed. It is by no means necessary to guard against such subjects or expressions as may relate immediately to their loss of sight ; on the contrary, it is better to use such as they occur, without any

remark. Blind persons, who have been well-accustomed to the
use of their other senses, acquire thereby such a knowledge of
things in general,—colours excepted,—that they are as able to
converse upon them as those who have their sight.

The Blind, even those who are born so, very commonly, in their
conversation, use the verb to "see," such as "I saw Mr. M., I have
seen a cocoa nut, &c.," and call different colours by their names,
which they have learnt by their intercourse with those who have
their sight. Therefore it is best to speak to them of colours as
you would to others, especially the colours of common things,
that they may have less difficulty in conversing about them with
those who see. In this way the child's memory will not only be
much strengthened, but also well stored with a fund of various
branches of knowledge, which will lead his reflecting mind and
fertile imagination to higher things, and develope the powers of
his understanding. Should he shew an inquisitive mind or a
desire for knowledge, check it not, but carefully encourage it.
Should he evince little or no such desire, then try, by easy
questions, to awaken his attention and reflection. Ask him to
describe, in his own way, any thing that he is well acquainted,
with, or describe something to him and let him say what the thing
is, which you are describing, &c. Easy riddles, puzzles, and such
things, are good practice ; and asking his *unreserved* opinion on
various subjects and occurrences, with which he is familiar, will
lead to some knowledge of his moral tendencies—a point of no
small importance.

*Section X.—Attending School, and School Instruction.*

A LARGE portion of what has been said applies not only to a *home
education*, but also to *school instruction ;* for a blind child, after it
has arrived at six or eight years of age, can attend any common
elementary school, for those who have their sight, with considerable benefit, if the teacher will only make proper allowance for the
disadvantage under which his pupil labours. Indeed, seeing
children might, on such opportunities, be taught some good moral
lessons, if the teacher will call their attention to the misfortune
of their blind companion, and the various means employed for
relieving it. Every little friendly attention they show to him—
whether it be by assisting him in his lesson, or by contributing to
his amusement, in the hours of recreation—will exercise some of
the best feelings of their nature, and make so strong an impression upon their minds that, in after life, they will, probably,
look back upon it with satisfaction and delight.

If we go further into the different branches of school routine we
shall find that the blind child will be quite as capable of learning
mental arithmetic, and spelling, when it is orally taught, as any of

his seeing schoolfellows. The form of the figures and letters is easily learnt by books which are embossed for the use of the Blind, and when the letters are not too large, they will be readily distinguished by a single touch of the finger. If no such books are at hand, the letters may be written, the wrong way (that is towards the left hand), and of moderate size, upon a sheet of thick paper, then let them be closely punctured, through the paper, with a pin or needle, and they will form letters, raised on the other side, so as to be readily legible by the touch. A third method of *writing*, for the Blind to read, by feel, is this :—Put into some gum water as much powdered chalk or magnesia, or lamp-black, as it will bear, without being too thick to flow. Dip a pen into this and write, as with ink—it may be made black by the addition of ink. If it be not sufficiently raised, at first, to be read by the touch, it may be gone over again as often as necessary, The blind child should have the fore-finger of the right hand directed over the letters, as if he were forming them, and he will thereby acquire a knowledge of their shape, &c. Letters may be made on separate bits of pasteboard, and a quantity of them put into different cells in a box. They may then be taken and placed in a frame with channels to fit them, to form words for learning to spell, &c. [Metal types, which are better for this purpose, may be had of Reed and Fox, type founders, London.] The advantage of such exercise, in improving the touch and fixing the attention, is greater than at first may be supposed.

For beginners in arithmetic the apparatus called the " Russian reckoning frame " will be found very serviceable, even for those who see, as well as the blind, and every teacher should be acquainted with its use. It may be procured at most toy shops. To use the frame or machine place it horizontally, so that the wires may lie with one end towards you ; then the beads (9 of which will be on each wire) on the right hand wire will represent the units, up to nine ; those on the second, represent the tens ; the third the hundreds ; the fourth the thousands, &c. Each wire being at least as long again as is necessary to hold the beads. Place all the beads at the farther ends, then bring down, on each wire, as many beads as will represent the number belonging to that wire, thus to represent 1861, bring down 1 on the right hand wire, 6 on the next, 8 on the third, and 1 on the fourth from the right hand ; when a cypher occurs, none are brought down, &c. With this machine, in the hands of a skilful teacher, amusement may be combined with instruction. Some use it with the wires placed horizontally, when the frame may be upright or lie flat : in that case the units will be on the upper wire, or the one farthest from you.

When anything is to be committed to memory, the Blind (if it be read to them) will equal, if not surpass those who see, in getting it off.

*Religious Instruction.*—The mind of a blind person is very readily impressed with a pious belief, and turns with gratitude to any one who will kindly unfold to him the truths of religion, to guide and console him in his dark passage through this life, and cheer him with the prospect of a better hereafter. If, in the school which he attends, the elements of Geometry should be taught, he will be able, by the touch, to comprehend, as well as those who have their sight, the forms of the various bodies presented to him, and the diagrams may be drawn on paper and punctured with a needle from the other side. Triangles, squares, &c., cut out of paper or pasteboard, will answer the purpose exceedingly well, or the paper may be laid upon something soft, as cloth, &c., and the figures drawn the reverse way with a stile or blunt point, which will raise them on the other side. Should there be instruction in Natural History, illustrated by the exhibition of natural products, he will be found fully capable of examining and understanding even the more delicate parts of plants, flowers, and living creatures, or stuffed specimens. Geography is also within the reach of the Blind, and will interest them much. Maps may be rendered available by puncturing the division lines, &c., as recommended for letters or geometrical figures. A large puncture for a city, finer ones for smaller towns, and a pressure with a blunt instrument for hills, &c.; or some of this may be done with the thickened gum water. Rivers or roads may be traced with a blunt point as before mentioned. A dotting wheel, such as is generally supplied in cases of drawing instruments, run over the lines on the back of the paper, will beautifully emboss diagrams, letters, maps, &c.

History is a very proper, interesting, and well-adapted, subject for the Blind, as it serves to enrich the memory and the understanding, and requires no other help for the study of it than a close attention. Should the parents of the blind child be in circumstances to enable them, out of school hours, to give him a little private instruction, by way of preparation for the school, they will thereby find his progress in learning much facilitated and increased. Of course all this should, as far as possible, have respect to his great inlet for information—*the sense of touch.*

Arithmetic * forms an important branch of education for the Blind, and it may be taught—to any extent—by means of boards full of holes, into which little pegs are to be placed, to represent the figures. The holes and pegs are pentangular, in some; square or octangular in others. Each peg has a small pointed projection at one end and two such projections at the other, and, as it can be placed, in the pentagonal holes, five different ways, with the one

* The plans here described for teaching Arithmetic are such as are in use in England, those described by Knie being more cumbrous and expensive, and not so fit for general use.

end up, and five with the other, every peg can thus be made to represent any one of the nine figures, and the cypher. These various boards may be seen and procured at most schools for the Blind, and can be better understood by inspection. Those with *octagonal* holes have square pegs, each of which can be placed in 16 distinct positions, consequently 16 different characters can be represented by them, enabling the pupil to perform operations in Algebra, involving not more than three unknown quantities. [These boards are made of gutta-percha, with type metal pegs, and may be had of Messrs. Pope and Son, 80, Edgware Road, London.] But it will always be desirable to practise the Blind in *mental* arithmetic, to some extent, before putting the board and pegs into their hands. One great object is to give to the Blind a clear notion of the mode pursued in teaching arithmetic to those who have their sight, and to explain fully to them the terms and expressions used in so doing. Arithmetic is an admirable exercise for the mind. Not less important is it, in some cases, to teach the Blind to *write*, in the common way, which is easily done with a black-lead-pencil between two raised lines, or, which is better, by laying a piece of black tracing paper upon the other and writing with a blunt point, by which means the letters will be formed on the white paper and remain permanent. Yet sometimes the Blind will not make much use of this acquirement, merely because they are not able to read what they have written. Stamps for making the aforesaid punctured letters are to be had at most of the Blind Schools in Germany, and at some in England. KNIE has contrived a convenient apparatus, of this kind, fitted up with the requisite letters, signs, &c., and it may be obtained at the School for the Blind, at Breslau, for 5 thalers—[about 15*s*. English].

For instruction in geography, the terrestrial globes of Dr. Zeune, of Berlin, are to be recommended. On these the land is represented higher than the water, and the hills still higher, so as to be very distinguishable by the touch. The same kind of globes, and also maps in the same embossed way, are to be had of Mr. Kummer, in Berlin, either with or without the addition of the names of places, &c. Lest the names should crowd these maps so as to render them difficult to make out, it is advisable to make a knot upon a piece of strong thread or string, and, with a needle pass it through the map, where any town may be, and on the back of the map, tie to the string a bit of card or parchment, with the name stamped upon it, in the punctured manner before named, so as to be legible by the touch. If only a *few* names are required on a large map, they may be pasted on the face near to the hole, and even when they are very numerous, if tied to the threads, the name wanted may be easily found, by placing the left hand on the face of the map, and the right hand under amongst the names. Then by drawing up the knot representing any town, the name attached to it on the back will readily be found, with the right hand, and may then be read.

Some knowledge of geometry is highly advantageous to blind persons, and should be taught in all cases, where it is practicable, not merely because it beneficially exercises and sharpens the mental faculties, but also because it furnishes the mind with useful information, supplies matter for contemplation, and is the best means of enabling the blind to understand descriptions of such bodies as may be either too large, or too small, to the examined by the touch.

The diagrams and figures in plain geometry may be made by drawing them on strong paper, and puncturing them through, from the back, in the same way as for letters, &c., or they may be drawn with the thickened gum-water before-mentioned. For solid geometry, as well as for spherical trigonometry, the author has contrived a collection of figures, &c., which suit equally for the blind and the seeing, and may be had for thirty thalers [about £4 10s. English]. But it should be particularly stated whether they are for the blind or those who see, as, when made for the latter only, the figures are not raised, or distinguishable by the touch, and therefore can only be used by such as have their sight. If, in the school, there should no instruction be given, in mechanical or natural knowledge, these things will serve for private education ; and, even with females, this sort of information should, by no means, be altogether neglected. In teaching history, &c., the names of places, dates, and such like may be impressed, (by the before-described stamps for letters,) either by the tutor or pupil, by way of exercise or repetition.

The Blind very readily acquire foreign languages, and the more they are taught the better,—provided they be well grounded in them,—as they can in after life become excellent teachers, not only of the Blind, but also of those who have their sight, and thereby earn a livelihood as tutors or governesses. Even so can they teach mental arithmetic, history, religion, and (by help of various ingenious contrivances) geography, geometry, mechanics, &c. One of the best Latin schools in Saxony is kept by a blind man, who is famed for well grounding his pupils in that language. Should there be a gymnasium (college) in the town, a clever blind person may visit or attend it, with advantage ; and if his friends are in circumstances to afford to let him have one or two boys who see (if of his own class the better), to read and write for him, he will benefit more than if he has only a tutor who could not spare much time to read to him, &c. For the wealthy blind, mental or intellectual acquirements are most suitable ; for the poor, mechanical operations. Music is desirable for both.

## Section XI.—*Instruction in Music.*

BLINDNESS seems to produce, what might be termed, a natural delight in music ; yet it is not every blind person who has a natural talent for learning it. Those who have their sight often fail to accomplish it, but the blind, *in general*, very readily acquire considerable proficiency in that art, from which they derive so much pleasure. The best test or proof of musical talent, in a blind child, is the practice of singing, by which it will soon be ascertained, whether or not he has a voice, or at least an ear for music. First sing to the child (if he has not already of himself begun to sing) some single note within the compass of his voice, (or give the note from some instrument,) sustaining it, and at the same time endeavour to cause the child to imitate it : should he fail to do so, but yet produce some other note, then let the teacher take *that* note, and sustain it, till his pupil has correctly sung it several times in succession. After this, two notes may be sounded, one after the other, and the child required to say which is the higher or lower. In this practice the notes should always be near to each other, as 2nd, 3rd, 4th, &c. If two notes (which differ only a whole or a half-tone) be sounded in succession, and the child can readily say which is the higher, or which is the lower, there is good ground for supposing that he has some ear for music, and likely to make progress in it.

NOTE.—A musical ear, like most other senses, is capable of great improvement by judicious treatment. Pupils who at first could not distinguish between two notes, a third apart, have, afterwards, as experience has shewn, been able to judge to the eighth part of a note or tone. Care must be taken not to over-strain the voice by attempting, at first, to reach very high notes.

The following observations and advice respecting the names and effects of single tones, the various scales, chords, &c., must be as strictly observed by the Blind as by those who have their sight. The blind pupil should be first made acquainted with the notes, and different keys in music, and this can be easily done by help of the thickened gum water, &c., by which notes may be made so as to be readily distinguished by the touch.* The "time" also must be taught, and the value of crotchets, quavers, &c., thoroughly understood. In each exercise, before proceeding to another, the pupil must know, and at once be able to name, each note, its value, &c. Particular care should be taken to form the notes correctly. Sometimes it happens that the child may have no voice for singing and yet possess a good ear for music ; such children will readily distinguish between notes played or sung by others, or

* In Glasgow several music books are published in embossed notes, which answer far better than making the notes of thickened gum water, &c. Also a selection of embossed Psalm tunes, with a table of the musical characters, notes, &c. To be had of Marsh, York.

imitate them by whistling, and thus evince their turn for *instrumental* music. If you find that your pupil has an ear for music, endeavour to teach him to play on some instrument. First make him well acquainted with his instrument and its different parts, and then shew him how the different notes are produced upon it—repeat to him the scale, and explain how it relates to that particular instrument. Let him practice the scale in the different keys, and neglect nothing that may tend to ground him well in the theory. In choosing a music master seek one that is not merely a good musician, but one who has also some idea of *method*, in his teaching, and able and inclined to enter into full explanations, for he should remember that his blind pupil has a *mind*, as well as hands and ears, to be instructed.

In teaching the blind, tunes, pieces of music, &c., there are two methods employed, the one is to *read* the notes to them, giving their names, value, place upon the stave, &c., the other is to *play* the notes to them on an instrument. The former takes more time, therefore, the latter is more generally used, for they acquire thereby a knowledge of the tone as well as the name of the note, and also of the time. In long pieces it is best to take only a few bars at once, and when these are learnt, to go on to a few more, till the whole be gone through. A little patience will, in this way, accomplish much. Of course, at first, very easy things should be chosen, and played over, in portions, to the pupil, as often as is necessary, for him to remember them. Great speed in learning is not desirable, at first. And, that playing by ear may not become a mere mechanical operation, let the pupil, after he has acquired any portion, give, orally, some account of the "time," value of the notes, &c., or try to sing them, if his voice will admit of it. This should be particularly attended to, and, if the teacher be not afraid of a little trouble, he will find the effect very satisfactory, as the pupil will thus acquire such a knowledge of the piece as to enable him to sing it over, as it were, in his mind, and to retain it.

It is not uncommon for the blind to be defective in "time." This arises chiefly from their having the piece in their memory, on which account the notes occur to them more readily than if they had to read them from paper, and therefore they, imperceptibly, quicken in playing, as those who have their sight generally do, when they play what they have "learnt by heart." This fault must be especially guarded against, and a correct idea of time or measure taught as early as possible. Let them be accustomed to compare crotchets with quavers, semiquavers, &c., and where the instrument will admit of it, to play them together as bass and treble, &c., and thus commence the practice of harmony. The before-mentioned naming and singing the notes (sol-fa-ing,) in the mind, as it were, will, here, have good effect. Transposition, or change from one key to another, should by no means be neglected, when the pupil is sufficiently advanced to perform this necessary exercise. It gives a knowledge of the keys, scales, &c., and affords an agreeable and useful practice. Begin with transposing single scales and chords, and practise this till the pupil can easily play or sing any short examples. This will be the time to explain something of the relations and connections of chords, &c. In learning instrumental music, the pupil should, where it can be done, begin with the piano. The fixed tones or notes of this instrument operate beneficially in educating a musical ear. Playing in full harmony gives a taste and feeling for the relations and connections of chords, &c. The great compass of this instrument affords the pupil an opportunity of practising the strength and activity of his fingers. In short, the piano is the best instrument for making a complete musician. In learning other instruments the following observations should be attended to :—If, in addition to a good ear, the pupil should possess physical activity, he may learn the violin, violoncello, &c., the bowing and fingering of which instruments require considerable dexterity. Should he not be so endowed he may choose a wind instrument, of wood or brass ; but, in that case, he should have good lungs and well-formed lips. And in these instruments he must learn to " tongue " certain notes, and when to take breath, which is very important. The *quality* of the tone should be studied ; and the mode of holding the instrument, as well as the position of the body, should in no case be neglected, more especially with the Blind, who have not the advantage of studying attitude or position by observing it in others. To give them grace and elegance requires particular and peculiar attention, but it is important. Where it is possible, let the tutor play to the pupil the piece to be learned, upon the instrument he has chosen and devoted himself to. Execution cannot be expected till the mechanical difficulties of the instrument are overcome. Unmeaning passages and pieces should never be chosen for exercise, as they mislead the imagination, and injure the musical taste of the pupil. Classical compositions will at all times serve to warm and exalt the feelings, and give a turn for the sublime and beautiful. When several blind pupils are to be taught together, such pieces and exercises should be chosen as include little solos upon each one's particular voice or instrument, as solo playing or singing gives the pupil confidence, and an opportunity of showing his taste and skill by playing.

Teachers who use irregular or unscientific accompaniments, do unpardonable mischief to their pupils, for the rules in music to be observed by the seeing are equally applicable to those without sight. The Blind may become organists, tuners of pianos ; teachers of singing, and of such instruments as they themselves have learnt to play upon. Also, members of quadrille bands, chorus singers, glee singers, &c. Boys may learn various sorts of instruments, but girls seldom play upon anything except the piano, organ, harp, guitar, or concertina. For the *poor* blind, music is somewhat dangerous, if they have not, with it, been taught some trade, or had their minds well cultivated, as it often leads them into bad company, or to go about as beggars. Even as respectable glee singers they are exposed to the temptation of drinking and other moral digressions. On account of this tendency to encourage vagrancy and irregular modes of living, in the dissolute and idle, music should be taught only as an amusement, or as a help towards a maintenance, in situations and societies, where the morals of the blind will be least in danger. That a good musical education ennobles the mind, ameliorates the feelings of the heart, and, at the same time, conduces, in some cases, to bodily exertion, in others, to manual dexterity, cannot be denied. Therefore musical instruction is to the blind, as it were, a sort of connecting link or medium between his intellectual and his mechanical education.

---

### Section XII.—*Handicraft peculiarly adapted for the Blind.*

Not only to themselves (as shewn in sections 3 to 8), but also to others, the blind can become highly useful. The girls (when young), in such things as winding yarn, fetching things for the use of the house, where this can be done without danger ; shelling peas and beans, paring potatoes and turnips, washing dishes, &c. When strong enough, they may make beds, and do other household work. The boys may fodder cattle, churn butter, pump water, &c. More opportunities of this kind occur in the country than in towns. Girls of delicate and feeble constitutions may plait straw, thread, whale-bone, hair, &c. ; spin, with spindle, and with the wheel ; knit with two or more needles ; also sewing may be done by them. Hesitate not to make blind boys (as you would the seeing) acquainted with knives, scissors, files, hammers, chisels ; and let them use them in making toys, &c.,—it will prepare them for using them afterwards in more important operations, as a means of subsistence. In most Institutions or Schools for the Blind the following branches have been carried to great extent, and have also been profitable :—Spinning, knitting in all its branches,— crochet work, making doileys, &c. ; netting of all kinds, in silk and other materials ; plaiting hair, ribbon weaving, making sash-line, list and leather shoes and boots ; straw plaiting, mats for dishes, ditto for the feet ; beehives, and mattresses of all kinds ; pasteboard boxes, of various sorts, basket work, from the coarsest to the finest kinds, in fancy patterns ; wood-turning, joinery, coopering, sawing, planing, &c. ; chairs bottomed with willows, reeds, cane, &c. ; brushes of various kinds ; whips, straps, twine, ropes ; clasps, hooks and eyes, wire covers for dishes, lattice, flower stands, file cutting, &c. Even more difficult work has been done by some clever blind persons, such as making clocks, musical instruments, cutting and polishing precious stones, carving in wood, &c. [In all these operations a leather finger-stall will be of great advantage if placed on one finger (usually the forefinger of the right hand) to protect it, and keep the touch as delicate as possible, for the purpose of feeling small things and reading embossed books.] Let teachers of the Blind remember that those who have their sight learn much from *seeing* their masters, or more clever companions, at work—this advantage the Blind are deprived of—everything must be *explained to them* in a peculiar manner. First shew them the article you are about to teach them to make in a complete state, together with the raw material ; explain the different parts of it, also the tools and manner of using them : then proceed, step by step, till you accomplish your object. This must be done by *guiding the hand* in every operation ; but the person guiding often holds it so fast that the Blind cannot perceive the effect he is producing either by his hand or the tool in it. This should be guarded against. Let the teacher (whether he has his sight or not) perform very slowly some work, and let the Blind lay his hand upon that of the teacher and examine and mark every movement of it, as well as of any instrument used in it, as he goes on, and he will soon be able to do the like himself. The instruction of the Blind in works of handicraft is at first difficult, and requires patience and thought, but the difficulty soon vanishes. In order to accomplish some of the before-named works, many peculiar plans have been devised, and many machines and implements contrived, which are in use in most schools for the Blind—others are done by the Blind in the same way as by the seeing. Basket makers, rope makers, &c., who have their sight, may, if they have heads and hearts in the right place, safely take blind boys as apprentices, if they have first been instructed in the elements of their trade in some blind school, as before directed. They would find them faithful and industrious labourers, and grateful pupils. This difficulty in teaching the blind ought by no means to deter persons from undertaking it, for, if they will only consider the importance of it, they will be encouraged to come forward in so good a work, not merely on account of any pecuniary advantage, but for the sake of the religious and moral influence which their precepts and instructions might have in promoting the future welfare of their sightless pupils. The Blind who have learnt a trade are thereby rendered the more cheerful, from a feeling that they can, in some degree, contribute to their own support ; are more reconciled to their fate, and more submissive to the will of God. The greatest act of charity you can do to needy blind children is to teach them a trade ; for by so doing you may save them from becoming common beggars, or a burthen to their friends. To " eat the labour of their own hands " is, to the

Blind, most gratifying and encouraging. You parents who have blind children, and suffer them, through neglect, to continue in idleness or fall into a state which may lead, perhaps, to beggary and immorality, forget not that you will have to give an account to God for a breach of duty to children who have a more than common claim upon your parental care and affection, which, if timely and properly applied, might prevent consequences deeply to be deplored. You who think that blind persons are incapable of learning to become useful members of society, read the accounts of remarkable blind persons, or visit schools for the blind, and you will soon see cause to change your opinion, and no longer remain in an error which must be injurious to your afflicted offspring. As an example of the mode of teaching here alluded to, take the threading of a needle. At first take a large bodkin, through the eye of which a small string will readily pass. Let the child take the string, with the end cut *short off*, and place it between the left thumb and forefinger, so that the end of the string may not come quite to the ends of his thumb and finger ; then let the child take with the right hand the bodkin, about a finger's breadth from the eye ; cause the eye to touch the thumb nail of the left hand (in order to ascertain its exact position) ; open a little the thumb and finger, between which the end of the string or thread is held ; press the eye of the bodkin between them against the end of the string, which will easily enter it ; open the thumb and finger a little more and thrust the string forwards, then close the thumb and finger of the left hand so as to hold the bodkin, while the string is drawn through, by the right thumb and finger. With very dull or unskilful children a wire may be at first used instead of a string, and a piece of wood or bone, with a somewhat larger hole bored through it. Instead of a bodkin they may put the string through large beads, buttons, &c. By degrees, with frequent trials, they may change the string for coarse thread, and the bodkin for a darning needle, and afterwards finer thread and needle as they become more expert. [Some thread needles No. 8 or 9, with the tongue !]

*Knitting* requires little apparatus and little room, and can be learned in any town or village. At first the child or pupil should use very strong needles somewhat pointed, and a thick flexible string or yarn. Let the teacher take two needles, and with them " cast on " 12 or 15 stitches and knit a few rounds, during which the blind girl should lay her hands upon those of the teacher and examine carefully, by feel, what she is doing and how she does it. Of course she must knit very slowly, and describe every part and movement as she proceeds, which the pupil should closely attend to. Then let the pupil try, holding one needle in each hand, and the thread over, and once round, the fore-finger of the right hand, and between the other fingers. The use of this will afterwards appear. Having done this let the pupil, with the left thumb-nail, separate from the rest the stitch nearest the end of the needle, or the last made, then slantingly, from the inside towards the outside, thrust the needle she has in her right hand through the stitch, and under the other needle ; now let her put the thread over the end of the needle (thus thrust through from the left towards the right), and draw the needle back, through the stitch, with the thread upon it, pointing it a little downwards to prevent the thread slipping off,—draw the stitch, which was first separated from the others, off the end of the left-hand needle, and a stitch is completed. This operation must be repeated for every stitch. By a little practice it will be easy to knit with four or five needles, and the most intricate work may be performed by the blind as well as by those who have their sight. Beads of various sorts may also be knitted in, with good effect, but they must be put upon the yarn before the knitting is begun. It is, perhaps, easier to knit with a sheath fastened to the waist, into which the near end of the needle with which the stitch is made is to be put, when three or more needles are to be used. Round knitting may then be taught without difficulty. Plaiting straw, &c., may also be taught by any one acquainted with the art.

*Section XIII.—A few Games at which the Blind may play, and even join in them with the seeing.*

*Dice and Dominoes.*—In these games the spots must be raised, by having small round-headed nails driven into the dice or dominoes, or the latter may be cut out of thick paste-board, and the dots punctured with a needle, which will raise a burr on the other side, easily distinguishable by the touch. Or, when very large, the dots or spots may be *sunk*, as in common cases, and yet be easily felt.

*Draughts.*—The draught board must have all the white squares raised about the twentieth of an inch. Half of the men have, in the middle, a little peg, which projects about a quarter of an inch ; the other half have holes in the middle, into which the pegs go, when " kings " are made, as, without the pegs, the upper one would be liable to be displaced by the blind, in feeling the state of the game.

*Chess* may be played on the same board ; but, for this purpose, each square must have a hole in the centre for the reception of a peg at the bottom of each piece. The white men or pieces are all pointed on the top, and the black ones rounded. The form in other respects may be according to taste.*

* There is, at present, a blind chess player who can play six games at once (that is, with six different players), w.thout touching any board. He knows the situation of every piece upon each of the boards, so that, should either of the boards, in any part of the game, be accidentally upset, the pieces can all be again put into their proper places, under his direction.

*Throwing the Ring.*
*Skittles or Nine Pins.*—A favourite game with the Blind.
*Cards.*—A pack of cards must be prepared for the blind, in the following manner. With a *fine* needle, pierce them through from the back, thus : for the *suit*, the punctures must be in the middle of the top ; one for hearts, two for spades, three for clubs, and four for diamonds. For the *value*, the right hand corner, at the top, must be pierced with dots in the form that counters or coins are placed to reckon the tricks at whist. For an ace, one dot or puncture. For a duce, two placed horizontally. For a trey, three dots placed horizontally. For the four, four dots placed horizontally. For the five, two horizontal and one over them, forming a triangle. For the six, three horizontal dots and one over the middle one. For the seven, two horizontal and one under (the five reversed). For the eight, three horizontal dots, with one under the middle one (the six reversed). For the nine, four dots in the form of a square. Ten, four dots in the form of a lozenge. Knave, two dots placed perpendicularly. Queen, three perpendicular dots. King, four perpendicular dots. Thus :—

|  |  |  |  |  |  |  |  |  |  |  |  |  |
|---|---|---|---|---|---|---|---|---|---|---|---|---|
| . | .. | ... | .... | .. | ... | : | ∴ | :: | ∵ | : | ⋮ | ⋮ |
| 1 | 2 | 3 | 4 | 5 | 6 | 7 | 8 | 9 | 10 | K | Q | Kg |

*Blind-man's Buff, Hide and Seek, Riding a Spring Horse, Swinging, &c. Riddles, Charades, &c., &c., &c.*

---

*Section XIV.—Particular views and observations relating to the Treatment and Education of the Blind, and to the care for their welfare.*

BLIND children should be taught to be very particular in attending to everything which demeanour, custom, or modesty, requires or forbids. But, as loss of sight shuts them out from many advantages, and makes divers plain and simple things, at first, difficult to comprehend, they require more patience and attention, on the part of the teacher, than those who see. Therefore, teach them how to dress and undress themselves ; how to attend to their various wants ; how to address people and express their obligations ; how to behave, at Church, at table, in company, &c. For example—When they speak to any one, they should always turn their face towards him ; when they yawn or cough, always put a handkerchief, or at least the hand, before their mouth, &c. Further, it is highly necessary that the Blind be taught not to sit in a crooked posture ; not to move about awkwardly ; not to keep their bodies, nor any part thereof in constant unnecessary motion ; not to have their heads drawn down between their shoulders ; not to keep the mouth open, when attending to anything ; not to make unseemly distortions of the features—not to thrust the finger into the eye-sockets,—a custom very common with the Blind. All these, and other bad habits, must be early attended to, and particularly guarded against—for it is misplaced indulgence, and false kindness, in parents to allow these things, as they tend to render their blind children, if not objects of ridicule to the thoughtless, at least less agreeable to their friends. Therefore let such habits be checked in the beginning, for it is much easier to prevent than to correct them. Since the Blind are deprived of such enjoyments as depend upon sight, it is not to be wondered at that they should, sometimes, have recourse to other and less desirable means of amusing themselves. Regular exercise and occupation are the most likely to prevent many disagreeable and perhaps injurious practices. Idleness (the beginning of most evils) will, if indulged in, produce and encourage habits which may affect their morals and mar their happiness. The Blind have less to distract their attention than others, consequently things take a deeper hold upon their minds, on which account it is doubly important to watch closely all their conduct, and guard against everything which may be hostile to good manners or to a virtuous course of life. They should be kept from all places where they would hear bad language, or bad sentiments, for their good memories will not only retain what they hear, but their lively and active imaginations will work upon it, so as, often, to endanger their principles. * * * Many persons, with the kindest motive, but not aware of its effect, will express pity for the Blind in their hearing. This ought especially to be avoided, as it painfully reminds them of their misfortune. Those who have been born blind, or have lost their sight at a very early age, are ignorant of many of the pleasures and advantages which they are deprived of, by want of sight—therefore it is most desirable, in their presence, not to speak of their situation as *unfortunate*, not to commiserate, *aloud*, their affliction. Through such mis-placed sympathy many blind persons are rendered dissatisfied with their lot, and become morose, who would, otherwise, be contented and happy. Those, who *see*, should never forget that blindness excludes very few *mental* enjoyments or advantages ; it is nearly confined to exterior ones, therefore such expressions of pity should be avoided, as no one likes to be constantly reminded of that which he would gladly forget. Expressions of this kind betray want of thought, if not of feeling.

It is a painful thing, to the Blind, to be laughed at on account of any little mistake they may make through want of sight,—this the young feel more than the old, and are more injured by it, as it discourages them from asking for information, or expressing their sentiments, with that freedom which is so necessary to their com-fort and advantage ; no benevolent person will be guilty of it.

D

Great injury is often done by *undue and injudicious praise,* and by (what appears to the informed blind absurd) the wonder and astonishment, so frequently expressed by those who have their sight, at their accomplishing many little works which are, to them, not really difficult, and if done by the seeing would be considered merely as ordinary operations. Such praise does harm, for it gives the better informed blind the idea that those, who see, think meanly of them and their capabilities, by praising mere trifles. This injudicious praise more especially affects the *young* and inexperienced blind, and frequently induces them to fancy that they are unusually clever ; thus they become vain, and dissatisfied, if they are not lauded for every trifling operation they perform. The blind have much need of *patience and perseverance* to enable them to overcome the difficulties which, on account of their deprivation, beset them on every side. To both these they should be well accustomed from their early years ; and neither, in their lessons nor in their work, should they be allowed to go to any new thing, till they well understand that which they are then about ; therefore it is most desirable (at first, at least,) not to put them to do anything which they are not likely to accomplish, for to have to give up things, as above their skill, only serves to discourage them. Furthermore, they should be accustomed to govern their passions and inclinations, and not let the allurements of sin take too deep hold upon their minds. Contentment, discreet openness towards others, readiness to oblige, becoming modesty, and faithfulness to any trust reposed in them, should be constantly inculcated. The character of the blind is, generally speaking, amiable and cheerful, often marked by stedfastness, justice, a great desire for knowledge, and a love of truth. When it is otherwise, it not unfrequently arises from the cold, and sometimes unkind, treatment which they occasionally experience from unthinking, or unfeeling, persons, who have their sight.

Should there be some ground to hope that the blind child might hereafter, by an operation, or otherwise, be restored to sight, it will still be desirable to educate him as if there were no such hope. For should a cure not be effected, he will then be in a worse condition than other blind children, who had been regularly trained to encounter the difficulties connected with their situation. Even in case of a successful operation he will, for want of education, be more backward than other seeing children ; for that which has been neglected in early years can seldom, if ever, be made up afterwards. It is *generally* more difficult to educate one who is born blind, or who became so at a very early period, than one who loses his sight at the age of eight or ten, or perhaps later, and retains a clear recollection of what he had been accustomed to see: for his knowledge of external objects will enable him to understand many explanations and descriptions, which those who are born blind can but imperfectly comprehend. Most of the observations in the foregoing sections will be equally applicable to blind adults, in learning trades, &c.—The erroneous notion that the blind are incapable of acquiring useful knowledge, is the chief cause of their being so often neglected in their childhood and youth ; and yet the direct contrary is little less dangerous to their welfare. For some people suppose that the Blind, *in consequence* of their misfortune, are endowed with extraordinary capabilities, and vainly think that, if they are educated in some one branch only, such as music, for example, they must, necessarily, be able to attain perfection in any other. This has already misled many teachers of the blind, even in public Institutions, where one branch of education predominates, and induced them to attempt too much, with pupils of only moderate abilities. The fault here manifestly arises from not well considering what the talents of the pupil are equal to,—whether he is likely to arrive at eminence in any particular branch, so as to do credit to himself, or gain a livelihood thereby. Sometimes, in public schools attention is chiefly paid to the affluent, or to the highly gifted, while those of only moderate abilities, or the poor, are culpably neglected. This ought not to be the case, for it is not right to develope the extraordinary talents of one, at the expense of numbers, who are only moderately endowed. The former are likely to become conceited, the latter discouraged.

There are many Asylums in which the Blind are provided for, during their whole life, but it is impossible that such Institutions can receive all who are fit objects for them. The care for a blind child does not cease with his youth. His parents—unless they are amongst the wealthy—must always feel great anxiety lest, in case he should survive them, they should not be able so to provide for him, as to ensure to him a comfortable subsistence, or at least to keep him from want. Those who can afford it, would do well to purchase for him an Annuity, which, at a comparatively small outlay, would afford him a maintenance, and secure him from being burdensome to his friends. This, in the case of blind daughters, is most desirable, in addition to what they may enjoy from any little testamentary bequest, official salary, or the profits of manual labour.

# APPENDIX.

*Short Biographical Sketches of some remarkable persons who were born Blind, or became so in their early years, selected, chiefly, from Klein's " Lehrbuch."*

*Jacob Brown,* born at Bruck, in Lower Austria, 1795, was the son of a carpenter, and lost his sight at three years old, by small pox. He was Klein's first pupil, and, in consequence of the progress he made in learning, the school at Vienna was founded in 1806. He learnt to read from raised letters, and to write, played the harp, acquired a good knowledge of geography, history, natural history, natural philosophy, and several other branches of education. He could knit, net, weave, make baskets, turn on the lathe, and was so expert a carpenter that he made tables, chairs, bedsteads, wardrobes, and other kinds of household furniture. He modelled animals and other things in wax (of a reduced size), and made himself a plate electrical machine, with which he amused himself. He arranged all his household affairs; sowed seeds in his garden, planted and grafted trees; gave instructions to other blind young men, in various occupations, and was so fully employed, all day, that time never hung heavy on his hands.

*Corsepius,* born at Passenheim, in E. Prussia, lost his sight when six years old, by the small pox. He modelled in wax, and made many machines, both in wood and metal.

*Frederick Gottlieb Funk,* of Nodau, in Switzerland, was born 1780, and, went quite blind at seven years old. He, without much assistance from others acquired sufficient knowledge, on various subjects, to enable him to become a teacher, not only of those who were blind, but also of those who had their sight. He contrived several methods and devised divers means of facilitating the education of the blind; amongst which were an arithmetic board, with holes, and pegs on the top of which the figures are worked in points, &c. Also, a writing-table, and a simple instrument for embossing letters, by which he could make all the Roman capitals on paper. He was a good musician, turned on the lathe, worked in wood and metals, in a way calculated to astonish those who saw him. For five years he was tutor to the children of a neighbouring clergyman, and in 1809 he was appointed a teacher in the blind school at Zurich, where his talents, patience, and industry, produced surprising effects upon his pupils. He may be looked upon as an example of what a blind man can effect, by his own perseverance and a little help from others.

*Joseph Gattermeyer,* born at Obritz, in Austria, in 1758, became blind in his third year. He foddered the cattle, drew water, cut wood, cleaned the house, and, for amusement, made children's waggons, bird-cages, &c. He worked in the field and vineyard, could thatch, hedge, make bricks, mend his shoes, and thread a needle. He made all the chairs, tables, &c., in his house; bought everything for his family, such as food, clothing, &c. Looked after the cellars of his brother, who was a wine and spirit merchant, and often acted as guide to strangers in the neighbourhood. He was a married man.

*Francis Gregor,* born blind, at Sternberg, in Moravia, in 1802, was a great proficient upon the harp, on which he played in public, when he was so young that it was necessary to set him and his harp upon a table, in order that he might be seen. He made great progress in different branches of knowledge, as well as in the theory and practice of music.

*Blind Jacob,*—his surname and time of birth not known,—was born at Netra, a Hessian village, and lost his sight, in the eighteenth month of his age, by the small pox. He acquired much knowledge in the village school when a boy, and, afterwards, endeavoured to compensate for his loss of sight by various simple contrivances, among which the following was one of his most important : He took staves of wood, about 30 inches long, and half-an-inch square, along these he cut, with a knife, certain marks or notches, which served him instead of letters or words. Each of these staves was thus notched, or written upon, as it were, on two sides, and recorded what he wished to remember, of what he had heard read or spoken. He cut these notches with great quickness, and from them he could read as from a book. All the staves which belonged to the same subject he tied together, forming, as it were, volumes, and distinguished them by certain signs, so that he could, at once, lay his hand upon the bundle he wanted to consult. Thus he formed a library of such bundles or volumes ; and when any book was mentioned which he had heard read, he could immediately take up the bundle containing his remarks upon it, and read them off quite fluently. He died in 1779. His curious staves fell into the hands of his relatives, who, not knowing their use or value, destroyed them.

*Joseph Kleinhanns,* born in 1777, lost his sight by small pox at 4½ years old. He was remarkable as a carver in wood. He made busts and statues from one foot high to the size of life. At the request of his countrymen he carved the figure of a Tyrolese soldier, 18 inches high, and gave such expression to the countenance as would have done credit to a *seeing* artist.

*Johann Knie*—[Author of the little work here translated]—was born at Erfurt in 1794, and was totally blinded, by the small pox, in his tenth year. He acquired much knowledge, in various branches of education, by attending schools for the seeing ; and at the age of 15 he entered the blind school at Berlin ; there, under the management and tuition of that able and benevolent man, Dr. Zeune, he made unusual progress, in learning, during the five years which he passed in that institution. He felt so great a desire to benefit his companions in misfortune, that he determined to devote himself to the education of the Blind. And, in order to fit himself for the task of teaching, he went to the University at Breslau, where for three years he studied, with great success, Mathematics, History, Geography, and whatever was necessary for the instruction of youth. His extraordinary memory was of the greatest use to him in acquiring the dead languages, which he did with great facility. He could repeat, almost verbatim, any lecture he had heard. In 1818 he prevailed upon twelve gentlemen to form themselves into a committee for establishing, in Breslau, a school for the Blind, which was opened in 1819, and in 1821 he became the director of it, and has continued to hold that appointment ever since, with credit to himself and advantage to the institution. His mild disposition and irreproachable conduct, together with his great acquirements, eminently qualify him for the discharge of the important duties which he has undertaken. He has translated several works connected with the blind, from different languages. He travelled, alone, through the greatest part of Prussia, Germany, &c., for the purpose of visiting the various schools and asylums for the blind, as well as other public institutions, and published an account of his journey in a very interesting 8vo. volume, entitled, *" Paeda-gogische Reise durch Deutschland, &c. in* 1847."

*John Kaferle* was born at Weiblingen, Würtemberg, in 1768. In his fourth year he became quite blind, from an arrow which struck him, whilst looking at archers practising. He soon showed extraordinary talents especially for Music and Mechanics. When he was five years old, some one gave him a common toy fiddle, on which he was soon able to play all the melodies with which he was acquainted. He then learned to play the guitar, and in a very short time surpassed his teacher. At 13 years old he made various implements, machines, and pieces of furniture, with such skill as to excite the admiration of all who saw them. In later years he made clocks, and invented a machine by which he could readily make the wheels, &c. At the age of 22 he made a piano-forte. Shortly after this his father's mill was burnt down by lightning, and when it was re-built he made most of the wheels, &c. He invented a peculiar kind of air-gun, but it was prohibited by the pol'ce. To relate all the extraordinary things which this wonderful man was able to perform would exceed the limits of this sketch, and appear almost incredible.

*John Fred. Niendorfer*, born in 1757, lost his sight by the small pox when he was three years old. He could not only clean but repair clocks, watches, and even repeaters!

— *Bunau*, daughter of a civil officer in Roda, was born about the year 1770, and may be looked upon as a pattern or example of all those who share her misfortune. She was blinded by the small pox in her third year. Her mental qualities were of a high kind, and she possessed superior natural talents, which she exercised in various ways, to lessen the severity of her misfortune, by useful occupation and innocent amusement. In order to communicate with her distant friends, she caused a large quantity of bits of paper, to be cut of the same size, and the letters of the alphabet written singly upon them. These she kept in a box of cells or divisions, like those in which printers put their types. When she wanted to write to any one, she took a needle and thread, and put upon it the different letters, in the order of the words she wished to communicate, putting a blank bit between every word. The receiver of this communication had only to draw the papers a little apart, and read them in the order in which they are placed upon the thread. She afterwards learnt to write with a pencil, of which she made great use; and she became unusually expert in various feminine occupations, as well as several mechanical ones. She was very poetical.

*Maria Theresia von Paradies*, born in 1759, lost her sight at three years of age. Her parents were persons of rank and fortune, and they spared no expense in cultivating her extraordinary talents, and procuring for her the various ingenious contrivances then known for facilitating the education of the Blind. She was a distinguished Musician, and as such visited nearly all the capitals and principal towns of Europe. Her disposition was mild and cheerful, her character altogether most amiable, and her manners easy and pleasing. She thought the opinion of the *seeing*, as to what was beautiful, could not be of much value, as so few of them agreed on that point. When she was at Paris she corresponded with her highly-educated blind friend Weissenberg, of Manheim. This becoming known to the never-to-be-forgotten Valentine Haüy, gave him the first idea of establishing a school for the general instruction of those deprived of sight, and hence arose that great and valuable Institution for the Blind, which does credit to Paris and to the French nation. M. T. von Paradies became an expert Arithmetician, through the use of the table or apparatus invented by the great Saunderson, the blind Professor of Mathematics in Cambridge. The Empress, Maria Theresa, was her godmother, and allowed her a yearly pension of 200 florins.

*Le Sueur*, born at Paris in 1776, was the first pupil of the first school for the blind,—the Paris School,—of which he afterwards became the manager.

*Von Golz*, blind at 13 years old, was a doctor of law, and professor in Königsberg.

*Paingeon*, born blind. Professor of Mathematics in Paris.

*Pfeffel*, the renowned poet, blind from his youth, was principal of the military school at Colmar, and afterwards established and conducted a school for those who had their sight.

*Schoenberger*, lost his sight at three years old, was born at Königsberg, and understood many of the living and dead languages; gave instructions in them, and discussed, with acuteness, many subjects, both in mathematics and philosophy.

*Griesinger*, of Worms, lost his sight at three years old; understood eight different languages, and was a popular preacher in Königsberg.

*Rolli*, born in Rome, studied science, especially physics and the higher mathematics.

To give even a short sketch of all the remarkable blind persons, of both sexes, would require a large volume. I have not given any account of the extraordinary blind persons in *England*, such as Moyes, Blacklock, Melcalf, Gough, Saunderson, Stanley, Strong, Lucas, Milton, &c., as they have been made known to the public by Wilson and others; but I hope the few I have noticed will be sufficient to encourage parents, who may have blind children, to give them the best education they can, and not to look upon them as burthensome, or a drawback upon their happiness, but regard their charge as a sacred duty, to those for whom God especially cares, inasmuch as he has pronounced a curse upon him who maketh the blind to " wander out of the way."—Deut. xxvii. 18.

### Additional Remarks.

NOTE.—Many poor persons who have blind children often endure great privations rather than seek parochial relief for their sightless offspring, under an impression that they shall, thereby, become *paupers* and lose certain privileges; but there is a clause in an Act passed in the reign of Wm. IV.,* which authorises parents to receive parish relief for blind, or deaf and dumb children, under sixteen years of age, without thereby becoming paupers, or forfeiting any privileges. This ought to be generally known, as it may prevent much unnecessary suffering.

Gymnastic exercises are very desirable for the blind, and they may enjoy the pleasure of running " at full stretch "—without danger.—in the following way : Let a post be fixed firmly in the centre of some grass plat; let the one end of a long cord be fastened to a ring, which turns round the post, and let the blind person take hold of the other end, and run round the post, keeping the cord tight. Perhaps it would be better if a long pole, like a capstan, were attached to the post, as in that case several may take hold of it, and run at the same time, the smaller ones being nearer to the centre.

A board of cork is very useful : Pins may be stuck in it, and a thread passed round them, so as to represent right-lined geometrical, and other figures, &c.

The blind acquire much information by attending common schools for the seeing. [See biography of Blind Jacob, page 36 ]

It is desirable that the blind, in doing rough work, should wear a " finger-stall," upon the finger they chiefly use in reading embossed books, examining minute objects, &c.. in order to preserve, as much as possible, the delicacy of touch. In reading it is best to use the fore-finger of the right hand to decipher the letters, while the others may be employed in ascertaining the length of the word, and whether (in the common alphabet) it ends with a letter which goes above the line, as b, d, l, &c., or one which goes below, as g, y, p, &c., as this will greatly facilitate the making out of the word, and enable the pupil to read more quickly. When the blind do not succeed in reading, in any alphabet, the fault is oftener with the teacher than the pupil. The blind are the best teachers of the blind in all things not requiring sight. In reading embossed books, it is desirable to place a piece of pasteboard between the page being read and the next, to prevent the letters of the under one being felt through the paper of the upper, which would produce confusion. With this the books get less injured, and last longer.

The blind often feel interested in reading inscriptions and epitaphs on grave-stones. Of course only those who have learnt the *common* letters.

Reading to the blind is always acceptable and profitable to them.

Hientzsch has given the following interesting table of the blind in Prussia ,

* 4th and 5th Wm. IV. c. 76, s. 56.

in the years 1846 and 1849, shewing the general decrease of the malady in that country in three years:—

| | Children under 15 years of age. | | Between 15 and 30. | | Above 30 years of age. | | Total. |
|---|---|---|---|---|---|---|---|
| | Males. | Females. | Males. | Females. | Ma'es. | Females. | |
| 1846. . | 451 | 371 | 706 | 674 | 4,015 | 3,788 | 10,005 |
| 1849. . | 441 | 326 | 770 | 635 | 3,900 | 3,507 | 9,579 |
| Result . | 10 | 45 | 64 | 39 | 115 | 281 | 426 |

## Head-work for the Blind.

THEY may be taught reading, writing, cyphering, geography, algebra, geometry, and other branches of the mathematics, with the sciences founded upon them; such as astronomy, mechanics, hydraulics, &c.. also history, natural history, theology, metaphysics, logic, grammar, languages, and philosophy, both natural and moral; may lecture in literature and science; study chemistry, modelling in clay, wax, &c.; teach schools, be parish clerks, conduct psalmody and other singing, &c.

## Hand-work which the Blind are capable of doing.

VARIOUS kinds of housework, such as making beds, washing, baking, rubbing furniture, turning mangles, carrying water, wood, &c.; churning, shelling peas, beans, &c.; taking care of linen; knitting, netting, sewing, crochet, lace, plaiting straw, hair, &c.; making doileys, mats for dishes, paper boxes, shoes, of list or leather; brush-making, wire-working, cutting files, sawing wood, drilling and filing iron, brass, &c.; joinering, turning, coopering, blowing bellows, ringing bells, playing organs, or other instruments; weaving cloth, mats, hearth-rugs, girths, &c.; making sash-line, whips, hooks and eyes, glass bugles, bead-work; make bricks, tiles, &c.; grind malt, coffee, pepper, colours, &c.; fringe-making, rope-making, spinning thread; tuning pianos; pounding in mortars; pumping water, cutting straw for horses, crushing beans, slicing turnips, carrots, &c., for cattle; basket-making, &c.

## A few general Rules which may be useful to those who have the care of Blind Children.

IT is of the greatest importance that blind children be religiously brought up; for, as they are deprived of many advantages which are open to those who have their sight, they stand in greater need of the promises and consolations of religion, which alone can afford them real comfort under their affliction, and enable them to bear it with patience and resignation. In giving religious instruction, the greatest care should be taken that every portion they are taught be fully and clearly explained to them, for, if left in doubt, they are very likely to fall into superstition on the one hand, or into scepticism on the other.

They should be treated in all things as much like the *seeing*, as circumstances will admit of, in order to render social intercourse with them agreeable and beneficial; for, as they have to live amongst those who see, they should have us many things in common with them as possible.

They should be accustomed to *activity* from their childhood, even if it be only for amusement. It, in a great measure, prevents their brooding over their misfortune, which not only injures their health, but unfits them for any useful exertion, either of mind or body.

Never assist them further than is necessary, in order to teach them to depend upon themselves. Jäger says "you cannot do a greater benefit to a blind child than to accustom him, as soon as may be, to do everything for himself as far as possible."

Encourage them to examine, carefully, everything which comes in their way, and not to be afraid of asking questions.

You need not be much concerned about any little hurt they may receive, from running against chairs, tables, &c., or in using certain instruments or tools, as such trifling accidents prevent greater, by teaching them caution.

In moving about a room, &c., should they take a wrong direction, it will be well to set them right *privately*, and to avoid as much as possible, where others are present, doing or saying anything to make them feel their dependence upon those who have their sight.

Amongst the many ingenious contrivances for facilitating the education of the blind, make choice of the *simplest*, and, as far as possible, such as are in use among those who see, when they are sufficient for your purpose; *and never depart from the common or beaten track, when that will lead to the object you have in view.*

Avoid giving utterance to feelings of pity or commiseration for the blind, in their presence, as it reminds them of their misfortune and gives them pain. Von Baczko (blind), relates the following anecdote:—"I was once sitting on a public seat, when a neighbour, whom I knew to have what is called a hunchback, joined me, and began to pity my misfortune, and to tell me of the pleasure I lost on account of my blindness, &c. I said Yes, it is a misfortune to be unlike other people. Possibly *you*, sometimes, have the unpleasantness of hearing unfeeling remarks made upon your deformity.—I had proceeded no further, when my crook-backed neighbour got up and, muttering some dissatisfaction, walked away."

When you meet blind persons whom you intend to address, always make yourself known to them, by mentioning your name, unless your voice is familiar to them,—it spares them the unpleasantness of doubt, as to who you are, and, to some extent, guides them in what they have to say in return.— Where there are several together, always make it known which of them you speak to, either by touching their hand or shoulder, or by mentioning their name, if you know it. For if they do not know which is spoken to, neither of them will venture to give an answer; and this often makes strangers go away with an unfavourable opinion of them,—perhaps thinking them stupid,—whereas the fault lies with themselves. A touch of the finger on the hand or arm is, to a blind person, what a smile is, to one who can see.

When you ask a blind person a question, and you receive an answer, always signify your agreement with it, or dissent from ; for if you go away in silence, you leave him in doubt whether or not his answer may have displeased you.

Do not ask blind persons if they have *heard* such and such a book read, but say, "have you *read* such and such a book, or have you *seen* Mr. A. or Mr. B., &c." It gives them the comfortable feeling that there is nothing so remarkable in their appearance as to direct attention to their misfortune.

Be careful how you *watch* blind persons,—unperceived, as you may suppose,—lest by smelling, hearing, or by feeling an impulse of the air, they detect your presence; in that case you will forfeit their good opinion. Also be very careful never, intentionally, to *deceive* them, even though you should think it for their good, for, if they find it out, it will tend to render them suspicious, and you will lose their confidence, never to regain it. Besides, it is not so easy to deceive them, as some may imagine; for as they have to depend upon *four* senses to do the duty of *five*, their discernment acquires an unusual degree of acuteness, which is extremely valuable to them, not only in their intercourse with others, but also in their education.

It is not necessary, in conversing with the blind, to avoid such subjects as relate to vision, &c., for, from frequently hearing things described, they will

E

form very good notions of them, and their lively imagination will supply useful representations of them.

Give them every possible opportunity of examining natural and artificial objects. Among the former may be reckoned specimens in geology, zoology, conchology, crystalography, metals, seeds, plants, flowers, fruits, wood, &c. Among the latter, various instruments, machines, money, weights, measures, cloth, articles of various manufactures, regular solids, such as cones, cubes, spheres, cylinders, &c.

When young, store their minds with extracts from the best authors, and especially from the Scriptures.

Never keep a pupil puzzling over things which he does not understand,—it only tends to make him less inclined to encounter difficulties. Always explain to him fully and clearly the *principles* on which he is acting, and lead him on by questions which he can easily answer, to those which are more difficult. *Success* will encourage him to greater efforts, but *defeat* will damp his ardour, and perhaps produce in him a dislike to learning.

Never praise him for *great talents*, but for industry, attention, perseverance, good conduct, and such other things as are under his control.

---

## Contemplations on the Blind.

WHO can read the annals of the Blind, or witness their privation, without the deepest interest in their welfare? Who can shut his ear against their rightful claims for succour and support? Or who, that is now blest with sight, can feel secure that he may never have to share their lot? To them, the outer world is all a blank! Their mortal life is veil'd in one perpetual night, and all around them pitchy darkness—"Dark amidst the blaze of noon!" Yet not in wrath has God thus closed one inlet to the mind, but in His wisdom, and for ends unknown to man. The blind do not behold the hand that administers to their relief; nor do they see the tear of sympathy which flows at their misfortune: but, when the voice of kindness or affection falls upon their ear, their hearts will bound with joy and turn, in grateful love, to that Almighty Being, "who tempers the wind to the shorn lamb." Though they cannot perceive the golden morn advance upon the mountains, nor mark the shades of night retiring from the vales, yet they listen to the matins of the lark, as though it were a voice from Heaven, inviting them to enter upon the new-born day, by lifting up their hearts in prayer to God who takes them under his peculiar care.* They look not upon the verdant landscape, bounded by the distant hills, and studded with "cloud-capt towers" or "heaven-directed spires," yet they can hear the hum of busy life—can feel the influence of the cooling breeze, and muse in calm enjoyment! They see not how the still evening closes on the drowsy world; they gaze not upon the brightness of the starry host, nor watch the fleeting clouds progressing through the moon's pale beams. Yet, though their outward senses are diminished, their minds are free to wander through the boundless realms of space, and open to receive the knowledge of that benignant God "whose goodness extends to every creature " and "whose tender mercies are over all His works."† The Blind, as well as those who have their sight, can ponder with delight upon the mighty operations of Nature, which their lively imaginations present, "to the mind's eye," in all their grandeur and perfection. Their hearts can glow with all the better feelings of humanity; they are capable of entering into social converse and enjoyments; can take their stand as useful members of society, and well sustain their part among their seeing brethren. At times, indeed, they, from

* Deut. xxvii. 18. Isaiah xlii. 16.
† Psalm cxlv.

the neighbouring steeple, hear the solemn knell, as if it were the voice of
friends departed, calling them to serious thoughts and holy contemplations.
This oftentimes produces, in the Blind, a tranquil resignation and points to
that true, clear, and inward, light, which cannot fail to animate their hopes,
and cheer their weary journey through this mortal life, to that all-glorious
land, where " they will rest from their labours," where their " sorrows will be
turned into joy," and where their eyes will be opened to behold their God!

T.

---

" Geniesse, was dir Gott beschieden.
Entbehre gern, was du nicht hast,
Ein jeder Stand hat seinen Frieden,
Ein jeder Stand hat seine Last."

GELLERT.

---

## BOOKS, ON THIS SUBJECT, IN ENGLISH.

Biography of the Blind. By James Wilson.
The Land of Silence and the Land of Darkness. By the Rev. B. G. Johns,
Chaplain of the Blind School, St. George's Fields.
The Sense Denied and Lost. By Thos. Bull, M.D. Edited by the Rev. B. G.
Johns, Chaplain of the Blind School, St. George's Fields.
Tangible Typography : or How the Blind Read. By Edmund C. Johnson,
Member of the Committee of the School for the Indigent Blind, &c.
The Blind of London. By E. C. Johnson, Esq.
Dr. Guillie's Work on the Blind, translated into English from the French.
Reports of the School for the Blind at Boston, U.S. By Dr. S. Howe.
Reports of the School for the Blind at Philadelphia. By Friedlander.
There is also, at Philadelphia, an English Dictionary, in 3 vols., 4to., Embossed
in the common or Roman Letters, for the Use of the Blind. Published by
the Directors of the Blind School at Philadelphia, under the super-
intendence of Professor Dunglison, M.D.
The Blind : their Capabilities, Condition, and Claims. By Alexander Mitchell
(himself blind). Honorary Secretary to the Society for Improving the
Social Position of the Blind. Wilton House, Walworth Road, London.
*By the Translator.* Diagrams of the first book of Euclid ; Embossed for the
Blind.
——— Selection of Psalm Tunes ; Embossed for the Blind.
——— Report on different Alphabets proposed for the use of the Blind,
written at the request of the Royal Scotch Society of Arts, Edinburgh,
and published in their Transactions.
——— Report on Printing for the Blind. Published in the Transactions of
the British Association for the Advancement of Science, &c.
——— Lecture on the education of the Blind, delivered at the Royal
Institution of Great Britain, an abstract of which is published in their
Transactions.
——— Paper on the Education of the Blind, and on the establishment of a
College for those of the opulent classes, read at the meeting of the Social
Science Society, at Liverpool.

*By the Translator.* A short sketch (translated from the German) of the Life of J. W. Klein, Founder and Director of the Blind School at Vienna.
——— The Relation of the Blind to the World around them. (Translated from the German.)

*It is to be regretted that the following works have not been rendered available in England by translation, as the excellent matter they contain will afford every necessary information and instruction for the guidance of those who have the management and education of the Blind.*

*Klein.* Lehrbuch zum Unterricht der Blinden.
——— Geschichte des Blinden Unterrichtes.
——— Anleitung Blinden Kindern, &c.
——— Jakob Braun.
——— Anstalten für Blinde.
——— Blinden Lieder.
——— Beschreibung eines gelungenen Versuches Blinden Kinder zur Burg; Brauchbarkeit zu Bilden.
*Rotermund.* Nachrichten v. einigen Blindgebornen, &c.
*Daniel.* An Regierungen, Eltern, und Lehrer, &c.
*Jäger.* Ueber die Behandlung welche Blinden Kindern, &c.
*Orell.* Blinden Anstalt in Zürich.
*Carton.* Le Sourd-Muet et l'Aveugle.
*Didero.* Lettres sur les Aveugles.
*Dolezálek.* Ansichten über die Erziehung der Zölinge eines Blinden Anstalt, &c.
*Hienzsch.* Ueber die Erziehung und den Unterricht der Blinden, &c.
*Georgi.* Geschichte der K. S. Blinden Anstalt zu Dresden.
*Struve.* Kurzer Unterricht für Eltern und Lehrer der Blinden.
*Zeune.* Belisar, oder über Blinde und Blinden Anstalten.
*Freudenberg.* Gründliche Hülfe für Blinde, &c.
*Baczko.* Ueber mich selbst und meine Unglücks-gefährten, die Blinden.

Also the works of *Knie, Düfau, Müller. Niboyet, Hirzel, Nageli, Koch, Wolke, Altorfer, Neudegg, Lachmann, Braille, &c. &c.*

LONDON : PRINTED BY WILLIAM CLOWES AND SONS, LIMITED, STAMFORD STREET AND CHARING CROSS.

www.ingramcontent.com/pod-product-compliance
Lightning Source LLC
Chambersburg PA
CBHW021559270326
41931CB00009B/1292